C. K. WILLIAMS

REPAIR

C. K. WILLIAMS's many honors include an award in literature from the American Academy of Arts and Letters and the PEN/Voelcker Career Achievement Award in poetry. His collection *Flesh and Blood* won the National Book Critics Circle Award; it and *The Vigil* were nominated for the Pulitzer Prize. *Misgivings*, Williams's memoir of his parents, was published in 2000. He teaches in the Writing Program at Princeton University, and lives part of the year in Paris.

T0057924

BY C. K. WILLIAMS

Lies

I Am the Bitter Name

With Ignorance

Sophocles' Women of Trachis (with Gregory Dickerson)

The Lark. The Thrush. The Starling. (Poems from Issa)

Tar

Flesh and Blood

Poems 1963–1983

The Bacchae of Euripides

A Dream of Mind

Selected Poems

The Vigil

Poetry and Consciousness: Selected Essays

Repair

Misgivings

REPAIR

C . K . WILLIAMS

REPAIR

FARRAR, STRAUS AND GIROUX

NEW YORK

Farrar, Straus and Giroux
18 West 18th Street, New York 10011

Copyright © 1999 by C. K. Williams
All rights reserved

Printed in the United States of America
Published in 1999 by Farrar, Straus and Giroux
First paperback edition, 2000

Many of the poems in this book have appeared in magazines and
journals: "Ice," "Shock," and "Risk" in Poetry; "The Train" and
"Droplets" in The Yale Review; "Archetypes," "House," and "Not
Soul" in The Ontario Review; "After Auschwitz," "The Lie," and
"Dirt" in The New Republic; "The Dress" in The Atlantic
Monthly; "Bone" in American Poetry Review; "The Poet" and
"Tender" in Tin House; "Glass," "Space," "The Nail," "The
Island," and "Swifts" in Salmagundi; "The Cup" and "Depths" in
The Threepenny Review; "Last Things" in Harper's; "Last
Things," "Canal," and "The Dance" in Frank; and "Invisible
Mending" in The New Yorker.

The Library of Congress has cataloged the hardcover edition as follows:
Williams, C. K. (Charles Kenneth), 1936–
Repair / C.K. Williams. — 1st ed.
p.   cm.
ISBN-13: 978-0-374-24932-8 (alk. paper)
ISBN-10: 0-374-24932-6 (alk. paper)
I. Title.

PS3573.I4483 R46 1999
811'.54 — dc21

98051901

Paperback ISBN-13: 978-0-374-52706-8
Paperback ISBN-10: 0-374-52706-7

www.fsgbooks.com

FOR OWEN

CONTENTS

REPAIR

That astonishing thing that happens when you crack a needle-awl into a
  block of ice:
the way a perfect section through it crazes into gleaming fault-lines, frac-
  tures, facets;
dazzling silvery deltas that in one too-quick-to-capture instant madly
  complicate the cosmos of its innards.
Radiant now with spines and spikes, aggressive barbs of glittering light, a
  treasure hoard of light,
when you stab it again it comes apart in nearly equal segments, both
  faces grainy, gnawed at, dull.

An icehouse was a dark, low place of raw, unpainted wood,
always dank and black with melting ice.
There was sawdust and sawdust's tantalizing, half-sweet odor, which, so
  cold, seemed to pierce directly to the brain.
You'd step onto a low-roofed porch, someone would materialize,
take up great tongs and with precise, placating movements like a lion-
  tamer's slide an ice-block from its row.

Take the awl yourself now, thrust, and when the block splits do it again,
  yet again;
watch it disassemble into smaller fragments, crystal after fissured crystal.
Or if not the puncturing pick, try to make a metaphor, like Kafka's
  frozen sea within:
take into your arms the cake of actual ice, make a figure of its ponderous
  inertness,
of how its quickly wetting chill against your breast would frighten you
  and make you let it drop.

Imagine how even if it shattered and began to liquefy
the hope would still remain that if you quickly gathered up the slithery,
    perversely skittish chips,
they might be refrozen and the mass reconstituted, with precious little of
    its brilliance lost,
just this lucent shimmer on the rough, raised grain of water-rotten floor,
just this single drop, as sweet and warm as blood, evaporating on your
    tongue.

T H E   T R A I N

Stalled an hour beside a row of abandoned, graffiti-stricken factories,
the person behind me talking the whole while on his portable phone,
every word irritatingly distinct, impossible to think of anything else,
I feel trapped, look out and see a young hare moving through the sooty
    scrub;
just as I catch sight of him, he turns with a start to face us, and freezes.

Sleek, clean, his flesh firm in his fine-grained fur, he's very endearing;
he reminds me of the smallest children on their way to school in our
    street,
their slouchy, unself-conscious grace, the urge you feel to share their
    beauty,
then my mind plays that trick of trying to go back into its wilder part,
to let the creature know my admiration, and have him acknowledge me.

All the while we're there, I long almost painfully out to him,
as though some mystery inhabited him, some semblance of the sacred,
but if he senses me he disregards me, and when we begin to move
he still waits on the black ballast gravel, ears and whiskers working,
to be sure we're good and gone before he continues his errand.

The train hurtles along, towns blur by, the voice behind me hammers
    on;
it's stifling here but in the fields the grasses are stiff and white with rime.
Imagine being out there alone, shivers of dread thrilling through you,
those burnished rails before you, around you a silence, immense,
    stupendous,
only now beginning to wane, in a lift of wind, the deafening creaking of
    a bough.

Often before have our fingers touched in sleep or half-sleep and enlaced,
often I've been comforted through a dream by that gently sensitive pres-
sure,
but this morning, when I woke your hand lay across mine in an awkward,
unfamiliar position so that it seemed strangely external to me, removed,
an object whose precise weight, volume and form I'd never remarked:
its taut, resistant skin, dense muscle-pads, the subtle, complex structure,
with delicately elegant chords of bone aligned like columns in a temple.

Your fingers began to move then, in brief, irregular tensions and releas-
ings;
it felt like your hand was trying to hold some feathery, fleeting creature,
then you suddenly, fiercely, jerked it away, rose to your hands and knees,
and stayed there, palms flat on the bed, hair tangled down over your
face,
until with a coarse sigh almost like a snarl you abruptly let yourself fall
and lay still, your hands drawn tightly to your chest, your head turned
away,
forbidden to me, I thought, by whatever had raised you to that defiant
crouch.

I waited, hoping you'd wake, turn, embrace me, but you stayed in your-
self,
and I felt again how separate we all are from one another, how even our
passions,
which seem to embody unities outside of time, heal only the most be-
nign divisions,
that for our more abiding, ancient terrors we each have to find our own
valor.
You breathed more softly now, though; I took heart, touched against you,

and, as though nothing had happened, you opened your eyes, smiled at
    me,
and murmured—how almost startling to hear you in your real voice—
    "Sleep, love."

We'd wanted to make France
but by dusk we knew we wouldn't,
so in a Bavarian town
just off the autobahn,
we found a room, checked in,
and went out to look around.

The place was charming: hushed,
narrow, lamp-lit streets,
half-timbered houses,
a dark-stoned church,
and medieval bridges
over a murmuring river.

I didn't sleep well, though,
and in the morning, early,
I took another stroll
and was surprised to realize
that all of it, houses,
bridges, all except

as far as I could tell
the sleeping church, were deft
replicas of what
they must have been before
the war, before the Allied
bombers flattened them.

At Auschwitz, there was nothing
I hadn't imagined beforehand.

I'd been through it in my mind
so much, so often, I felt
only unutterably weary.
All that shocked me was

to find the barracks and bleak
paths unoccupied,
and the gas and torture chambers,
and the crematoria;
so many silent spaces,
bereft, like schools in summer.

Now, in a pleasant square,
I came on a morning market;
farmers, tents and trucks,
much produce, flowers,
the people prosperous,
genial, ruddy, chatty,

and it was then there arose
before me again the barbed
wire and the bales of hair,
the laboratories and
the frozen ash. I thought
of Primo Levi, reciting

Dante to the all but dead,
then, I don't know why,
of the Jewish woman, Masha,
of whom Levi tells

how, when she'd escaped,
been informed on, caught,

and now was to be hanged
before the other prisoners,
someone called out to her,
"Masha, are you all right?"
and she'd answered, answered, answered,
"I'm always all right."

A village like a stage set,
a day's drive back
that other place which always
now everywhere on earth
will be the other place
from where one finds oneself.

Not risen from its ruins
but caught in them forever,
it demands of us how
we'll situate this so
it doesn't sunder us
between forgivenesses

we have no right to grant,
and a reticence
perhaps malignant, heard
by nothing that exists,
yet which endures, a scar,
a broken cry, within.

In those days, those days which exist for me only as the most elusive
      memory now,
when often the first sound you'd hear in the morning would be a storm
      of birdsong,
then the soft clop of the hooves of the horse hauling a milk wagon down
      your block

and the last sound at night as likely as not would be your father pulling
      up in his car,
having worked late again, always late, and going heavily down to the cel-
      lar, to the furnace,
to shake out the ashes and damp the draft before he came upstairs to fall
      into bed;

in those long-ago days, women, my mother, my friends' mothers, our
      neighbors,
all the women I knew, wore, often much of the day, what were called
      "housedresses,"
cheap, printed, pulpy, seemingly purposefully shapeless light cotton
      shifts,

that you wore over your nightgown, and, when you had to go to look for
      a child,
hang wash on the line, or run down to the grocery store on the corner,
      under a coat,
the twisted hem of the nightgown, always lank and yellowed, dangling
      beneath.

More than the curlers some of the women seemed constantly to have in
      their hair,

in preparation for some great event, a ball, one would think, that never
    came to pass;
more than the way most women's faces not only were never made up
    during the day,

but seemed scraped, bleached, and, with their plucked eyebrows, scarily
    mask-like;
more than all that it was those dresses that made women so unknowable
    and forbidding,
adepts of enigmas to which men could have no access, and boys no con-
    ception.

Only later would I see the dresses also as a proclamation: that in your
    dim kitchen,
your laundry, your bleak concrete yard, what you revealed of yourself was
    a fabulation;
your real sensual nature, veiled in those sexless vestments, was utterly
    your dominion.

In those days, one hid much else, as well: grown men didn't embrace
    one another,
unless someone had died, and not always then; you shook hands, or, at a
    ball game,
thumped your friend's back and exchanged blows meant to be codes for
    affection;

once out of childhood you'd never again know the shock of your father's
    whiskers
on your cheek, not until mores at last had evolved, and you could hug
    another man,

then hold on for a moment, then even kiss (your father's bristles white
and stiff now).

What release finally, the embrace: though we were wary—it seemed so
audacious—
how much unspoken joy there was in that affirmation of equality and
communion,
no matter how much misunderstanding and pain had passed between
you by then.

We knew so little in those days, as little as now, I suppose, about healing
those hurts:
even the women, in their best dresses, with beads and sequins sewn on
the bodices,
even in lipstick and mascara, their hair aflow, could only stand wringing
their hands,

begging for peace, while father and son, like thugs, like thieves, like Ro-
mans,
simmered and hissed and hated, inflicting sorrows that endured, the
worst anyway,
through the kiss and embrace, bleeding from brother to brother into the
generations.

In those days there was still countryside close to the city, farms, corn-
fields, cows;
even not far from our building with its blurred brick and long shadowy
hallway
you could find tracts with hills and trees you could pretend were moun-
tains and forests.

Or you could go out by yourself even to a half-block-long empty lot, into
    the bushes:
like a creature of leaves you'd lurk, crouched, crawling, simplified, sav-
    age, alone;
already there was wanting to be simpler, wanting when they called you,
    never to go back.

THE BLOW

I saw a man strike a beggar,
a rank, filthy, though not,
truly, insufferable beggar.
He had touched the man, though,
from behind, to stop him,
which startled the man,

so he blindly swept out
his fist, not thinking—
but didn't that make it worse?—
and hit the beggar, harder
than he'd have meant to
if he'd meant to, on the chest.

He knew at once, I saw,
he'd made a mistake;
the beggar, as tipsy
as he was, was insulted,
indignant, but did the man
regret what he'd done

for the sake of the dignity
of the beggar, or for the years
he'd tried to attain
innocence, all for naught
now, or because, really,
he was a little afraid?

The beggar was shouting,
the man wondered whether
to offer him money,

but he guessed the beggar
would lord it over him,
so he looked angry instead.

Walking faster, the beggar
haranguing him still,
the man suddenly saw himself
and the beggar as atoms,
nullities, passing beside
one another, or through.

How we toil, he mused,
from this aimless hour
to that, from one intractable
quandary to the next, until
we're left only a horrible
fear of our own existence.

Which, he remembered,
a famous thinker thought once,
as the image rose in him
of a youth he'd seen in a madhouse,
". . . entirely idiotic, sitting
on a shelf in the wall."

"That shape am I,"
the sage despaired,
beholding his own mind
flickering desperately over
the great gush of the real,
to no end, no avail.

B O N E

An erratic, complicated shape, like a tool for some obsolete task:
the hipbone and half the gnawed shank of a small, unrecognizable ani-
   mal on the pavement in front of the entrance to the museum;
grimy, black with tire-dust, soot, the blackness from our shoes, our ink,
   the grit that sifts out of our air.

Still, something devoured all but this much, and if you look more
   closely,
you can see tiny creatures still gnawing at the shreds of decomposing
   meat, sucking at the all but putrefying bone.

Decades it must be on their scale that they harvest it, dwell and generate
   and age and die on it.
Where will they transport the essence of it when they're done?
How far beneath the asphalt, sewers, subways, mains and conduits is the
   living earth to which at last they'll once again descend?
Which intellect will register in its neurons the great fortune of this ex-
   ceptional adventure? Which poet sing it?
Such sweetness, such savor: luxury, satiety, and no repentance, no regret.

But Maman won't let you keep it.
"Maman, please . . ."
"It's filthy. Drop it. *Drop it! Drop it! Drop it!*"

Furiously a crane
in the scrapyard out of whose grasp
a car it meant to pick up slipped,
lifts and lets fall, lifts and lets fall
the steel ton of its clenched pincers
onto the shuddering carcass
which spurts fragments of anguished glass
until it's sufficiently crushed
to be hauled up and flung onto
the heap from which one imagines
it'll move on to the shredding
or melting down that awaits it.

Also somewhere a crow
with less evident emotion
punches its beak through the dead
breast of a dove or albino
sparrow until it arrives at
a coil of gut it can extract,
then undo with a dexterous twist
an oily stretch just the right length
to be devoured, the only
suggestion of violation
the carrion jerked to one side
in involuntary dismay.

Splayed on the soiled pavement
the dove or sparrow; dismembered
in the tangled remnants of itself
the wreck, the crane slamming once more

for good measure into the all
but dematerialized hulk,
then luxuriously swaying
away, as, gorged, glutted, the crow
with savage care unfurls the full,
luminous glitter of its wings,
so we can preen, too, for so much
so well accomplished, so well seen.

I always knew him as "Bobby the poet," though whether he ever was one
    or not,
someone who lives in words, making a world from their music, might be
    a question.

In those strange years of hippiedom and "people-power," saying you were
    an artist
made you one, but at least Bobby acted the way people think poets are
    supposed to.

He dressed plainly, but with flair, spoke little, yet listened with genuine
    attention,
and a kind of preoccupied, tremulous seriousness always seemed to ab-
    sorb him.

Also he was quite good-looking, and mysterious, never saying where he'd
    come from,
nor how he lived now: I thought he might be on welfare, but you didn't
    ask that.

He'd been around town for a while, had dropped from sight for a few
    months when
one evening he came up to me in the local bookstore; I could see he
    hadn't been well.

He looked thin, had a soiled sling tied on one arm, the beret he usually
    wore was gone,
and when I turned to him he edged back like a child who's afraid you
    might hit him.

He smiled at himself then, but without humor; his eyes were partly
    closed, from dope,
I guessed, then changed my mind: this seemed less arbitrary, more pur-
    poseful.

Still, he had to tilt his head back a little to keep me in focus in his field
    of vision:
it was disconcerting, I felt he was looking at me from a place far away in
    himself.

"Where've you been, Bobby?" I asked. He didn't answer at first, but
    when I asked again,
he whispered, "In the hospital, man; I had a breakdown . . . they took me
    away there."

Then he subsided into his smile, and his silence. "What happened to
    your arm?"
He dipped his shoulder, his sling opened, and cradled along his arm was
    a long knife.

"That looks dangerous," I said; "I need it," he came back with, and the
    sling came closed.
I was startled. Did he think someone was out to hurt him? Might he
    think it was me?

He never stopped looking at me; his agitation was apparent, and not re-
    assuring;
we'd been friendly, but I didn't know him that well. "Where's your
    book?" I asked finally.

He'd always carried an old-fashioned bound accountant's ledger, its
    pages scrawled
with columns of poems: his "book," though as far as I knew no one but
    he ever read it.

Again no response; I remember the store was well-lit, but my image of
    him is shadow;
the light seemed extracted from his presence, obliterated by the mass of
    his anguish.

Poets try to help one another when we can: however competitive we are,
    and we are,
the life's so chancy, we feel so beleaguered, we need all the good will we
    can get.

Whether you're up from a slum or down from a carriage, how be sure
    you're a poet?
How know if your work has enduring worth, or any? Self-doubt is almost
    our definition.

Now, waiting with Bobby, I could tell he'd had enough of all that, he
    wanted out;
that may have explained his breakdown, but what was it he expected
    from me?

I was hardly the most visible poet around; I'd published little, didn't give
    readings,
or teach, although, come to think of it, maybe that's just what Bobby was
    after.

Someone once said that to make a poem, you first have to invent the
poet to make it:
Bobby'd have known I'd understand how the first person he'd devised
had betrayed him.

Bobby from nowhere, Bobby know-nothing, probably talentless Bobby:
wasn't that me?
I'd know as well as he did how absurd it could be to take your trivial self
as the case.

But if Bobby'd renounced poetry, what was my part to be? To acknowl-
edge it for him?
Flatter him? Tell him to keep on? I might well have, but not without
knowing his work.

Then it came to me that his being here meant more than all that—it was
a challenge;
Bobby wanted to defy me, and whatever he'd taken into his mind I rep-
resented.

The truth is I was flattered myself, that it was me he'd chosen, but there
was that knife.
Though the blade was thin, serrated, to cut bread, not tendon or bone, it
still was a knife,

it could hurt you: despite myself, I felt my eyes fall to its sorry scabbard,
and as I did,
I could see Bobby'd caught my concern: he seemed to come to attention,
to harden.

Though he still hadn't threatened me quite—he never did—I knew now
      I was afraid,
and Bobby did, too: I could sense his exaltation at having so invaded my
      emotions;

an energy all at once emanated from him, a quaver, of satisfaction, or an-
      ticipation:
"This is my poem," he might have been saying, "are you sure yours are
      worth more?"

Then the moment had passed; it was as though Bobby had flinched,
      though he hadn't,
torn his gaze from mine, though it clung, but we both knew now nothing
      would happen,

we both realized Bobby's menace was a mask, that it couldn't conceal his
      delicacy,
the gentle sensitivity that would have been so useful if he'd been able to
      keep writing.

He must have felt me thinking that, too; something in him shut down,
      and I wondered:
would he take this as a defeat? Whose, though? And what would a vic-
      tory have been?

He turned then and without a word left, leaving me stranded there with
      my books
while he drifted out into the rest of his life, weighed down with his eva-
      sions, and mine.

I never found out what he came to in the end; I've always kept him as
   "Bobby the poet."
I only hope he didn't suffer more rue, that the Muse kept watch on her
   innocent stray.

These things that came into my mind,
that were unbearable, unthinkable.
Certain visions I suppose they could be called,
abominations that afflicted me with agony.

To think of them even now requires awful effort.
Like the hero going into battle
needing four strong men to lift his eyelids.
The unforgiving eyelids of my memory.

Like Perseus, the Gorgon in his mirror-shield,
how he could strike and not be turned to stone.
The stone slabs in my mind. All they hide.
All I've tried so to forget which stays in me.

Even, once, a head; it only matters whose to me.
A head hacked off, set bleeding on a table.
I had thought that only warriors, only Perseus,
could do these things. And yet it glared at me.

Though I knew it was my mind that had done
this thing, mind reeled away in agony.
The agonizing plasma consciousness can be.
Stone. Slabs of stone. Eyelids. Memory.

DROPLETS

Even when the rain falls relatively hard,
only one leaf at a time of the little tree
you planted on the balcony last year,
then another leaf at its time, and one more,
is set trembling by the constant droplets,

but the rain, the clouds flocked over the city,
you at the piano inside, your hesitant music
mingling with the din of the downpour,
the gush of rivulets loosed from the eaves,
the iron railings and flowing gutters,

all of it fuses in me with such intensity
that I can't help wondering why my longing
to live forever has so abated that it hardly
comes to me anymore, and never as it did,
as regret for what I might not live to live,

but rather as a layering of instants like this,
transient as the mist drawn from the rooftops,
yet emphatic as any note of the nocturne
you practice, and, the storm faltering, fading
into its own radiant passing, you practice again.

A tall-masted white sailboat works laboriously across a wave-tossed bay;
when it tilts in the swell, a porthole reflects a dot of light that darts to-
wards me,
skitters back to refuge in the boat, gleams out again, and timidly retreats,
like a thought that comes almost to mind but slips away into the general
glare.

An inflatable tender, tethered to the stern, just skims the commotion of
the wake:
within it will be oars, a miniature motor, and, tucked into a pocket, life
vests.
Such reassuring redundancy: don't we desire just such an accessory, faith
perhaps,
or at a certain age to be comforted, not daunted, by knowing one will re-
ally die?

To bring all that with you, by compulsion admittedly, but on such a slen-
der leash,
and so maneuverable it is, tractable, so nearly frictionless, no need to
strain;
though it might have to rush a little to keep up, you hardly know it's
there:
that insouciant headlong scurry, that always ardent leaping forward into
place.

R I S K

Difficult to know whether humans are inordinately anxious
about crisis, calamity, disaster, or unknowingly crave them.
These horrific conditionals, these expected unexpecteds,
we dwell on them, flinch, feint, steel ourselves:
but mightn't our forebodings actually precede anxiety?
Isn't so much sheer heedfulness emblematic of *desire*?

How do we come to believe that wrenching ourselves to attention
is the most effective way for dealing with intimations of catastrophe?
Consciousness atremble: might what makes it so
not be the fear of what the future might or might not bring,
but the wish for fear, for concentration, vigilance?
As though life were more convincing resonating like a blade.

Of course, we're rarely swept into events, other than domestic tumult,
from which awful consequences will ensue. Fortunately rarely.
And yet we sweat as fervently
for the most insipid issues of honor and unrealized ambition.
Lost brothership. Lost lust. We engorge our little sorrows,
beat our drums, perform our dances of aversion.

Always, "These gigantic inconceivables."
Always, "What will have been done to me?"
And so we don our mental armor,
flex, thrill, pay the strict attention we always knew we should.
A violent alertness, the muscularity of risk,
though still the secret inward cry: What else, what more?

The way you'd renovate a ruined house, keeping the "shell," as we call it,
    brick, frame or stone,
and razing the rest: the inside walls—partitions, we say—then stairs,
    pipes, wiring, commodes,
saving only . . . no, save nothing this time; take the self-shell down to its
    emptiness, hollowness, void.

Down to the scabrous plaster, down to the lining bricks with mortar
    squashed through their joints,
down to the eyeless windows, the forlorn doorless doorways, the sprung
    joists powdery with rot;
down to the slab of the cellar, the erratically stuccoed foundation, the
    black earth underneath all.

Down under all to the ancient errors, indolence, envy, pretension, the
    frailties as though in the gene;
down to where consciousness cries, "Make me new," but pleads as
    pitiably, "Cherish me as I was."
Down to the swipe of the sledge, the ravaging bite of the pick; rubble,
    wreckage, vanity: the abyss.

N A K E D

Pissing out the door of a cottage
in an after-squall wind before dawn
in the tame hill country of Wales,
farms everywhere, fences and hedgerows,
but still enough strangeness, precipitous
pastures, patches of woods shadowing
tangles of one-car-wide lanes,
to take you out of yourself for a time,

so, naked under the low lintel,
an unaffrighting darkness before you,
so much of a washed-clean breeze
with so many temperate pulses and currents
of sleek, sensitive air languorously
touching across then seemingly through you,
how not delight to imagine dawn's
first wash moving through you as well,

barns, trees, and crouched shrubs
blockily coming to themselves within you;
then cockcrow, birds chirring
awake, and the silence, too, within
and without, as you turn away, leaving
the old patched door ajar
to breathe in the last wisps of night,
the already headily fragrant field-scents.

I'd have thought by now it would have stopped,
as anything sooner or later will stop, but still it happens

that when I unexpectedly catch sight of myself in a mirror,
there's a kind of concussion, a cringe; I look quickly away.

Lately, since my father died and I've come closer to his age,
I sometimes see him first, and have to focus to find myself.

I've thought it's that, my precious singularity being diluted,
but it's harsher than that, crueler, the way, when I was young,

I believed how you looked was supposed to *mean*,
something graver, more substantial: I'd gaze at my poor face

and think, "It's still not there." Apparently I still do.
What isn't there? Beauty? Not likely. Wisdom? Less.

Is how we live or try to live supposed to embellish us?
All I see is the residue of my other, failed faces.

But maybe what we're after is just a less abrasive regard:
not "It's still not there," but something like "Come in, be still."

A pair of battered white shoes have been left out all night on a sill across
the way.
One, the right, has its toe propped against the pane so that it tilts oddly
upwards,
and there's an abandon in its attitude, an elevation, that reminds me of a
satyr on a vase.

A fleece of summer ivy casts the scene into deep relief, and I see the
creature perfectly:
surrounded by his tribe of admiring women, he glances coolly down at
his own lifted foot,
caught exactly at the outset of the frenzied leaping which will lift all of
them to rapture.

The erotic will diffused directly into matter: you can sense his menacing
lasciviousness,
his sensual glaze, his delight in being flagrant, so confidently more than
merely mortal,
separate from though hypercritically aware of earthly care, of our so
amusing earthly woe.

All that carnal scorn which in his dimension is a fitting emblem for his
energy and grace,
but which in our meager world would be hubris, arrogance, compensa-
tion for some lack or loss,
or for that passion to be other than we are that with a shock of longing
takes me once again.

DREAM

Strange that one's deepest split from oneself
should be enacted in those banal and inevitable
productions of the double dark of sleep.
Despite all my broodings about dream,
I never fail to be amazed by the misery
I inflict on myself when I'm supposedly at rest.

Rest? In last night's dream my beloved announced to me,
and to others in the dream as well, that her desire was . . .
to not limit her range of sexual choice.
I implored her, but she wouldn't respond.
Why would characters in one's own dream
share with the waking world such awful unknowability?

Dreams are said to enact unfulfilled needs,
discords we can't admit to ourselves,
but I've never been able to believe that.
I dream pain, dream grief, dream shame,
I cry out, wake in terror:
is there something in me that *requires* such torment?

There used to be books of dream:
every dream had symbolic meaning.
And the old Chinese believed
that dreams implied their reversal:
a dream of travel meant you'd stay home,
to dream of death meant longer life.

Yes, yes! Surely my beloved in my dream
was saying she loved only me.

The coolness in your eyes, love, was really heat,
your wish to range was your renewal of allegiance;
those prying others were you and I ourselves,
beholding one another's fealty, one another's fire.

Mad dreams! Mad love!

What was going through me at that time of childhood
when my mother drinking her morning coffee would drive me wild with
      loathing and despair?
Every day, her body hunched with indignation at having had to leave its
      sleep,
her face without its rouge an almost mortal pale,
she'd stand before the stove and wait until the little turret on the coffee-
      pot subsided,
then she'd fill her cup and navigate her way across the kitchen.

At the table, she'd set the cup down in its saucer, pour in milk, sit,
let out a breath charged with some onerous responsibility I never under-
      stood,
and lift the cup again.
There'd be a tiny pause as though she had consciously to synchronize
      her mouth and hand,
then her lips would lengthen and reach out, prehensile as a primate's
      tail,
and seem to *grasp* the liquid with the sputtering suctioning of gravity im-
      perfectly annulled.
Then, grimacing as though it were a molten metal she was bringing into
      herself—
always grimacing, I'd think: did she never know what temperature the
      stuff would be?—
she'd hold about a spoonful just behind her teeth before she'd slide it
      thickly down.

Thickly, much too thickly:
she must have changed its gravity in there to some still more viscous,
      lava-like elixir.

Then there'd be a grateful lowering of her shoulders.
Also then her eyes would lift to focus on a point beyond my head
as though always then a thought had come to her that needed rarer
   ranges of reflection.
She'd do that twice, all that always twice, and put the coffee down.
In its porcelain cauldron, the military-brownish broth would sway—
was her passion for it going to make it boil again?—and finally come to
   rest.

. . . As I never came to rest, as I had to watch, I knew the interval by
   heart,
her hand come down to it again, her head lower to it again,
that excruciating suction sound again, her gaze loosening again.
I'd be desperate, wild, my heart would pound.
There was an expression then, "to tell on someone": that was what I
   craved, to *tell* on her,
to have someone bear witness with me to her awful wrong.
What was I doing to myself? Or she to me?
Oh, surely she to me!

My love gives me some wax,
so for once instead of words
I work at something real:
I knead until I see emerge
a person, a protagonist;
but I must overwork my wax,
it loses its resiliency,
comes apart in crumbs.

I take another block:
this work, I think, will be a self;
I can feel it forming, brow
and brain; perhaps it will be me,
perhaps, if I can create myself,
I'll be able to amend myself;
my wax, though, freezes
this time, fissures, splits.

Words or wax, no end
to our self-shaping, our forlorn
awareness at the end of which
is only more awareness.
Was ever truth so malleable?
Arid, inadhesive bits of matter.
What might heal you? Love.
What make you whole? Love. My love.

S P A C E

The space within me, within which I partly, or possibly mostly exist:
so familiar it is yet how little I know it, I'm not even sure of its volume;
sometimes it expands behind me like a wing, sometimes it contracts,
and while the world is often in it, it's rarely wholly congruent with it.

I'm not even certain when or why the world happens to appear there,
in a way that means something, brings with it more than my perceptions
at that instant, something that arrives with an insistence, a *friction*,
so that I have to move myself aside within myself to make a place for it.

If this space, at any rate, were a room, its color would be beige, or
        umber,
with fleetings of gold, not the gold of icons, but paler, less emphatic:
when my eyes first close there's a momentary darkening there as well,
sometimes the dimness smolders more intensely, almost to blood red.

Reestablishing myself in myself like this always comes to pass,
it seems it can't not come to pass, but an effort is needed, too,
something like faith: my vision rolls back through the bell of the skull,
all my ordinary thoughts are deferred, time becomes purely potential,

then clumps of light, glowing, pulsing patterns stutter in, then images,
usually of where I am just then, then others, then I hear my breath,
feel my body, become aware of thoughts and language; but even then,
the unexpected can occur: right now, a sharp, rolling, planetary horizon.

Such a strange interval: I wonder if this is what the last, indivisible
        instant
before death might be, before the absolutely unluminous absence.

To open one's tangible eyes just then, as I do now: light, shapes, color! Close again; darkness without end, but wait, still glow, still sentience: bliss.

TANTRUM

A child's cry out in the street, not of pain or fear,
rather one of those vividly inarticulate
yet perfectly expressive trumpet thumps of indignation:
something wished for has been denied,
something wanted *now* delayed.

So useful it would be to carry that preemptive howl
always with you; all the functions it performs,
its equivalents in words are so unwieldy,
take up so much emotive time,
entail such muffling, qualifying, attenuation.

And in our cries out to the cosmos, our exasperation
with imperfection, our theodicies, betrayed ideals:
to keep that rocky core of rage within one's rage
with which to blame, confront, accuse, bewail
all that needs retaliation for our absurdly thwarted wants.

Not soul,
not that tired tale anyway about preliterate
people believing cameras would extract
their spiritual essence, nothing so obvious,

but what is it I feel has been stripped,
stolen, negated, when I look out across
this valley of old farms, mist, trees,
a narrow, steep-banked brook,

and have the thought take me that all this
is a kind of reservation, a museum,
of land, plants, houses, even people —
a woman now, crossing a field —

that it all endures only by the happenstance
of no one having decided to "develop" it,
bring in a highway from the turnpike,
construct subdivisions, parking lots, malls?

Not soul,
soul is what religions believed subsumes
experience and will, what philosophers
surmised compels us to beauty and virtue,

is what even the most skeptical still save
for any resolving description of inner life,
this intricately knotted compound
which resists any less ambiguous locution.

How imagine so purely human a term
applying to things, to the rushing brook
which follows the slant of soil beneath it,
the mist functioned by the warmth of air,

even the houses to be torn down or crowded
into anonymity according to patterns
which have no discernible logic, certainly
nothing one mind might consider sufficient?

Not soul,
but still, anthropomorphism or not,
the very shape and hue and texture of reality,
the sheen of surface, depth of shadow,

seem unfocused now, hollowed out,
as though the pact between ourselves and world
that lets the world stand for more than itself
were violated, so that everything I see,

the lowering clouds, the tempered light,
and even all I only bring to mind, is dulled,
despoiled, as though consciousness no longer
could distill such truths within itself,

as though a gel of sadness had been interposed
between me and so much loveliness
so much at risk, as though a tear
had ineradicably fixed upon the eye.

I'm on a parapet looking down
into a deep cleft in the earth
at minuscule people and cars
moving along its narrow bottom.
Though my father's arms are around me
I feel how far it would be to fall,
how perilous: I cringe back,
my father holds me more tightly.
Was there ever such a crevice?
No, I realized much, much later
we were on an ordinary building
looking down into a city street.

A picture book: desert sunlight,
a man and woman clad in sandals,
pastel robes, loose burnooses,
plying a material like dough,
the man kneading in a trough,
the woman throwing at a wheel.
Somehow I come to think they're angels,
in heaven, fashioning human beings.
Was there ever such a story?
No, the book, at Sunday school,
showed daily life in the Bible,
the people were just making jars.

Just jars, and yet those coils of clay,
tinted light to dark like skin,
swelled beneath the woman's hands
as I knew already flesh should swell,

and as I'd know it later, when,
alone with someone in the dark,
I'd close my eyes, move my hands
across her, and my mouth across her,
trying to experience an ideal,
to participate in radiances
I passionately believed existed,
and not only in imagination.

Or, with love itself, the love
that came to me so readily, so
intensely, so convincingly each time,
and each time ravaged me
when it spoiled and failed, and left
me only memories of its promise.
Could real love ever come to me?
Would I distort it if it did?
Even now I feel a frost of fear
to think I might not have found you,
my love, or not believed in you,
and still be reeling on another roof.

TREE

One vast segment of the tree, the very topmost, bows ceremoniously
    against a breath of breeze,
patient, sagacious, apparently possessing the wisdom such a union of
    space, light and matter should.

Just beneath, though grazed by the same barely perceptible zephyr, a
    knot of leaves quakes hectically,
as though trying to convince that more pacific presence above it of its
    anxieties, its dire forebodings.

Now some of the individual spreads that make up the higher, ponderous,
    stoic portion are caught, too,
by a more insistent pressure: their unity disrupted, they sway irrationally;
    do they, too, sense danger?

Harried, quaking, they seem to wonder whether some untoward response
    will be demanded of them,
whether they'll ever graze again upon the ichor with which such benign
    existences sustain themselves.

A calming now, a more solid, gel-like weight of heat in the air, in the tree
    a tense, tremulous subsiding;
the last swelling and flattening of the thousand glittering armadas of sun-
    light passing through the branches.

The tree's negative volume defines it now; the space it contains con-
    tained in turn by the unmoving warmth,
by duration breathlessly suspended, and, for me, by a languorous sense
    of being all at once pacified, quelled.

K I N G

1

A tall, handsome black man, bearded, an artist, in nineteen sixty-eight,
  in Philadelphia,
you're walking down Market Street two days after Martin Luther King's
  murder
on your way to the memorial service scheduled that morning near the
  Liberty Bell.
Thirty years later, and I can still picture you there: you're walking fast,
  preoccupied,
when suddenly a police car swerves over the curb in front of you, block-
  ing your way.

And I can see the two policemen, both white, cold, expressionless, glar-
  ing at you:
a long moment passes, then I see you looking over your shoulder, turn-
  ing away,
moving towards the street, to the back of the squad car, passing behind it
  off the curb,
around it to the sidewalk on the other side and continuing down Market
  again,
to Nineteenth, then right to Rittenhouse Square where someone's wait-
  ing for you.

When you see the person (he's white, like the policemen), you don't say
  anything;
though you'd made an appointment not an hour ago to go to the service
  together,
you don't even glance at him again until he runs after you, calling for
  you to wait.

You stop to talk to him then, but only long enough to tell him in a harsh,
low voice
everything that had happened with the policemen, then a few hard sen-
tences more.

2

Maybe my trying to relive this with you should stop there; this after all is
your story,
but something still feels unresolved between us, as so much does in our
culture.
I've heard black friends say that in some ways race matters were easier
then,
at least then the prejudice was out in the open, you knew where you
were:
even the police were only the most visible edge of a hardly covert white
racism.

But if the police were a symbol of something else, they were brutal
enough at it.
You could, if you were black, man or woman, be beaten to death by po-
licemen.
You could, at a cop's whim, be arrested for "disturbing the peace," or "re-
sisting arrest,"
which meant you'd done nothing, but had been battered badly enough
for it to show,
necessitating if not an excuse then a reason, which incidentally added to
your sentence.

Back then, too, even if you could afford a good lawyer, who might get you off,
  if the police were angry enough, you had reason to fear that in the bus from jail
  to the courtroom, you'd be raped, gang-raped, and no one would dare say a thing.
  All that had to have come to your mind as you stood, that idling squad car before you,
  the cops inside it with their clubs and guns, impassive, their eyes challenging, hard.

3

They'd have known when they'd spotted you where you were going; everyone was.
  And they'd have seen that you were confident, full of yourself: an "uppity nigger."
  However they'd have put it to themselves, they'd have believed that by insulting you
  they could denigrate King with you, debase what he'd stood for, demonstrate to you
  that if you thought he had released you from the trap of history you were deluded.

But there would have been even more they'd have wanted to be sure you understood,
  were ready to break their fists on you, maim or kill you so that you'd understand:

that their world would prevail, that authority, power, and absolute physi-
cal coercion
with no ethical dimension whatsoever must and will precede all and re-
solve all
and break everything down again and again into an unqualified domin-
ion of force.

All that would have passed between you in an instant, what came next,
though,
would have driven their rage to a level where you knew the situation
might explode:
it was their suspicion, and your certainty, that even if they did apparently
intimidate you,
they couldn't make you renounce in yourself the conviction of your
moral worth,
the inextinguishable truth that would supersede even what might seem
submission.

4

Wasn't that what would have made you know you'd have to turn and go
around them?
Surely your fury outstripped your fear, but didn't you make a truce with
them, and a wager?
The truce was your walking away and their acceptance of that as a sign of
compliance;
the wager, on their part, was that in your pretense of capitulation there'd
be uncertainty,
that one day you'd have to forgive yourself for your humiliation, and
wouldn't be able to.

And wasn't the wager on your side that though you might be hurt by your
seeming yielding,
the lesion of your doubt, your shame and possible self-accusations would
be outweighed
by knowing that nothing would have justified letting them exert their
thuggery on you,
that, no matter what they believed, they wouldn't, couldn't have negated
your anger?
But wouldn't your surrender have scorched you? Wasn't that what you
were saying to me?

*Don't tell me you know what I feel, and don't give me that crap about be-
ing with us,*
*you wouldn't know how to be with us, you don't know the first thing about
us.*
*For three hundred years we've coddled you, protected your illusions of in-
nocence,*
*letting you go on thinking you're pure: well you're not pure, you're the
same as those pigs.*
*And please, please, don't tell me again you can understand because you're
a Jew.*

5

A black man, a white man, three decades of history, of remembering and
forgetting.
The day was Good Friday: after a long winter, the first warm, welcoming
odors of spring.
People flowed to Independence Hall Park from all directions, everyone
was subdued;

if there were tensions, they were constrained by our shared grief; we held
   hands.
The night before, though, in some cities there were riots: gunfire, sol-
   diers, buildings burning.

Sometimes it's hard to know why they stopped: I often think if I were
   black in America,
I might want to run riot myself with the sheer hypocritical unendingness
   of it all:
a so-called politics of neglect, families savaged, communities fractured
   and abandoned.
Black man, white man: I can still see us, one standing stricken, the other
   stalking away;
I can still feel your anger, feel still because it's still in me my helpless de-
   spair.

And will you by now have been able to leave behind the indignities and
   offense
of both halves of that morning? Isn't that what we're supposed to do in
   our country;
aren't we given to believe our wounds will heal, our scars fade, our in-
   sults be redeemed?
Later, during the service, when the "overcome" anthem was sung, I
   started to cry;
many others in the crowd around were crying, black and white, but I
   couldn't see you.

OWEN: SEVEN DAYS

for Owen Burns, born March 5, 1997

Well here I
go again into my
grandson's eyes

seven days
old and he knows
nothing logic tells me

yet when I
look into his eyes
darkish grayish blue

a whole tone
lighter
than his mother's

I feel myself almost
with a *whoosh*
dragged

into his consciousness
and processed
processed processed

his brows knit
I'm in there now
I don't know

in what form but
his gaze hasn't
faltered an instant

though still his
brows knit and
knit as though to

get just right
what I am no
what I'm thinking

as though to get
what I'm thinking
just exactly right

in perplexity perhaps
his brows knit
once again

perhaps because
of how little
inscrutability

with which the
problem of me
is presented

not "Who are you?"
but more something
like "Why?

Why are you? Out
there? Do you
know?"

then his eyelids
start to flutter
time to sleep

and once again with
something like
another *whoosh*

I'm ejected back
out into my
world

bereft? no
but for an instant
maybe just a little

lonely just a
little desolated
just for a while

utterly confounded
by the sheer
propulsive

force of
being taken
by such love

Wouldn't it be nice, I think, when the blue-haired lady in the doctor's
    waiting room bends over the magazine table
and farts, just a little, and violently blushes, wouldn't it be nice if intesti-
    nal gas came embodied in visible clouds
so she could see that her really quite inoffensive *pop* had only barely
    grazed my face before it drifted away?

Besides, for this to have happened now is a nice coincidence because not
    an hour ago, while we were on our walk,
my dog was startled by a backfire and jumped straight up like a horse
    bucking and that brought back to me
the stable I worked on weekends when I was twelve and a splendid
    piebald stallion who whenever he was mounted

would buck just like that, though more hugely, of course, enormous,
    gleaming, resplendent, and the woman,
her face abashedly buried in her *Elle* now, reminded me I'd forgotten
    that not the least part of my awe
consisted of the fact that with every jump he took the horse would pow-
    erfully fart, *fwap, fwap, fwap,*

something never mentioned in the dozens of books about horses and
    their riders I devoured in those days.
All that savage grandeur, the steely glinting hooves, the eruptions driven
    from the creature's mighty innards:
breath stopped, heart stopped, nostrils madly flared, I didn't know if I
    wanted to break him or be him.

In a tray of dried fixative in a photographer friend's darkroom,
I found a curled-up photo of his son the instant after his death,
his glasses still on, a drop of blood caught at his mouth.

Recently, my friend put a book together to commemorate his son;
near the end, there's a picture taken the day before the son died;
the caption says: "This is the last photo of Alex."

I'm sure my friend doesn't know I've seen the other picture.
Is telling about it a violation of confidence?
Before I show this to anyone else, I'll have to ask his permission.

If you're reading it, you'll know my friend pardoned me,
that he found whatever small truth his story might embody
was worth the anguish of remembering that reflexive moment

when after fifty years of bringing reality into himself through a lens,
his camera doubtlessly came to his eye as though by itself,
and his finger, surely also of its own accord, convulsed the shutter.

As one would praise a child or dog, or punish it,
as one would chastise it, or hit it, *hit* it;
as one would say, *sit, sit down, be still*:
so don't we discipline ourselves, disparage,
do as thoughtlessly unto ourselves?

As one would tell a lie, a faithless lie,
not with good intention, to obviate a harm,
but just to have one's way, to win, *prevail*:
so don't we deceive ourselves,
and not even know we are?

A self which by definition cannot tell
itself untruths, yet lies, which, wanting
to tell itself untruths, isn't able to, not then,
and would like sometimes not to know
it's lied, but can't deny it has, not then.

And our righteousness before ourselves,
how we're so barbarous towards ourselves,
so mercilessly violate ourselves;
as one would never, with a loved one, harm,
never, with a dear one, strike, not *strike*.

As one would with an enemy, implacable,
as one would with an animal, intractable,
as one would with a self which savagely resists:
this amputating, this assailing, this self-slashing.
As one would lie, as one so fervently would lie.

Some dictator or other had gone into exile, and now reports were com-
ing about his regime,
the usual crimes, torture, false imprisonment, cruelty and corruption,
but then a detail:
that the way his henchmen had disposed of enemies was by hammering
nails into their skulls.
Horror, then, what mind does after horror, after that first feeling that
you'll never catch your breath,
mind imagines—how not be annihilated by it?—the preliminary tap,
feels it in the tendons of the hand,
feels the way you do with *your* nail when you're fixing something, mak-
ing something, shelves, a bed;
the first light tap to set the slant, and then the slightly harder tap, to em-
bed the tip a little more . . .

No, no more: this should be happening in myth, in stone, or paint, not
in reality, not here;
it should be an emblem of itself, not itself, something that would *mean*,
not really have to happen,
something to go out, expand in implication from that unmoved mass of
matter in the breast;
as in the image of an anguished face, in grief for us, not us as us, us as in
a myth, a moral tale,
a way to tell the truth that grief is limitless, a way to tell us we must al-
ways understand
it's we who do such things, we who set the slant, embed the tip, lift the
sledge and drive the nail,
drive the nail which is the axis upon which turns the brutal human
world upon the world.

C A N A L

The almost deliciously ill, dank, dark algae on the stone of its sides,
the putrid richness of its flow which spontaneously brings forth refuse,
dead fish, crusts, condoms, all slowly surging in its muck of gruel,
under the tonnage of winter sky which darkens everything still more,
soils the trash, fruit, paper, dead leaves, water, impossibly still more.

Yet trudging, freezing, along beside it, I seem taken by it, to be of it,
its shape, its ooze; in the biting wind it and I make one single thing,
this murky, glass-hard lid with gulls fixed in it lifting and falling,
this dulled sheet, dense as darkness, winding by indifferent buildings,
we compose a single entity, a unity, not as fanciful speculation

but as though one actually might be the sentient mind of something,
as though only watching this indolent swell would bring into me
all that ever touched it, went across, perished and dissolved in it,
all caught lymph-like in this mortal trench, this ark, this cognizance;
a craving spirit flung across it, a tranquil stillness deep within it.

T H E   D A N C E

A middle-aged woman, quite plain, to be polite about it, and somewhat
      stout, to be more courteous still,
but when she and the rather good-looking, much younger man she's with
      get up to dance,
her forearm descends with such delicate lightness, such restrained but
      confident ardor athwart his shoulder,
drawing him to her with such a firm, compelling warmth, and moving
      him with effortless grace
into the union she's instantly established with the not at all rhythmically
      solid music in this second-rate café,

that something in the rest of us, some doubt about ourselves, some sad
      conjecture, seems to be allayed,
nothing that we'd ever thought of as a real lack, nothing not to be ad-
      mired or be repentant for,
but something to which we've never adequately given credence,
which might have consoling implications about how we misbelieve our-
      selves, and so the world,
that world beyond us which so often disappoints, but which sometimes
      shows us, lovely, what we are.

Have I told you, love, about the experience
I used to have before I knew you?
At first it seemed a dream—I'd be in bed—
then I'd realize I was awake, which made it—
it was already frightening—appalling.

A dense, percussive, pulsing hum,
too loud to bear as soon as I'd hear it,
it would become a coil of audible matter
tightening over me, so piercing
I was sure I'd tear apart in it.

I'd try to say a word to contradict it,
but its hold on me was absolute,
I was paralyzed; then, my terror
past some limit, I'd try again: this time
I'd cry out aloud, and it would stop.

Trembling, I'd come to myself, as,
the night of your tests, I came shuddering
awake, my fear for you, for both of us,
raging more terribly through me
than that vision of annihilation ever did.

It was like the desolate time before you:
I couldn't turn to you for reassurance
lest I frighten you, couldn't embrace you
for fear I'd wake you to your own anxiety,
so, as I had then, I lay helpless, mute.

The results were "negative"; now
I'll tell you of those hours in which my life,
not touching you but holding you,
not making a sound but crying for you,
divided back into the half it is without you.

Glorious morning, the sun still mild on the eastward hills, the hills still
    hushed;
only sometimes will a placeless voice find its way across the softly sleep-
    ing valley,
a slightly higher wave rise and wash in sighing over the stony beach.

So pleasant in such peace the way self inhabits its perceptual containers,
luxurious to descend so insouciantly from the inwardly armored helmet
    of thought;
consciousness dilates, there's a feeling of lubrication, acceleration,

my attention, as though freed of me, darts from a here which often isn't
    here,
to a there which usually remains resolutely an *away*; darts now from a
    white house
to an even whiter church up behind it, then down across a thistled slope

before it lifts abruptly, captured by the apparition of a single yellow
    flower petal
·soaring in a magnifying gush of light unwaveringly *upwards*, towards the
    firmament.
A sign? To reinforce the fittingness with which vision and its contents co-
    incide?

Now a burly, gray-white, rather short-winged gull lifts into the square of
    window
and with a visibly potent muscling of its pinions banks from sight. An-
    other sign?
Of more strenuous felicities? But if one believed such things, what
    wouldn't be a sign?

What about the fisherman out on his boat? What of the slowly moving
    boat itself?
How productive mind can seem, wheeling through such doing-
    something doing-nothing,
how pure its feeling of achievement in these world-spun strandings of
    connection.

But now comes an intimation of distraction; might the moment be al-
    ready being lost?
No matter: let the swaying cypress, the ever-sweetening breezes be their
    own reprieve.
Another swell sweeps across the still-calm bay; everything ripples, every-
    thing holds.

My grandmother is washing my mouth
out with soap; half a long century gone
and still she comes at me
with that thick, cruel, yellow bar.
All because of a word I said,
not even said really, only repeated,
but *Open*, she says, *open up!*
her hand clawing at my head.

I know now her life was hard;
she lost three daughters as babies,
then her husband died, too,
leaving young sons, and no money.
She'd stand me in the sink to pee
because there was never room in the toilet.
But, oh, her soap! Might its bitter burning
have been what made me a poet?

The street she lived on was unpaved,
her flat two cramped rooms and a fetid
kitchen where she stalked and caught me.
Dare I admit that after she did it
I never really loved her again?
She lived to a hundred, even then.
All along it was the sadness, the squalor,
but I never, until now, loved her again.

Why this much fascination with you, little loves, why this what feels like,
 oh, hearts,
almost too much exultation in you who set the day's end sky ashimmer
 with your veerings?
Why this feeling one might stay forever to behold you as you bank,
 swoop, swerve, soar,
make folds and pleats in evening's velvet, and pierce and stitch, dissect,
 divide,
cast up slopes which hold a beat before they fall away into the softening
 dusk?
That such fragile beings should concoct such sky-long lifting bends
 across the roofs,
as though human work counted for as little as your quickly dimming in-
 tersecting cries.

Tiniest dear ones, but chargers, too, gleaming, potent little coursers of
 the firmament,
smaller surely, lighter, but with that much force, that much insistence
 and enchantment;
godlings, nearly, cast upon the sky as upon a field of thought until then
 never thought,
gravity exempting from its weary weight its favorite toy, oh, you, and its
 delights, you and you,
as you hurl yourself across the tint of sinking sunlight that flows behind
 you as a wake of gold.
And the final daylight sounds you wing back to your eaves with you to
 weave into the hush,
then your after-hush which pulses in the sky of memory one last beat
 more as full dark falls.

Three women old as angels,
bent as ancient apple trees,
who, in a storefront window,
with magnifying glasses,
needles fine as hair, and shining
scissors, parted woof from warp
and pruned what would in
human tissue have been sick.

Abrasions, rents and frays,
slits and chars and acid
splashes, filaments that gave
way of their own accord
from the stress of spanning
tiny, trifling gaps, but which
in a wounded psyche
make a murderous maze.

Their hands as hard as horn,
their eyes as keen as steel,
the threads they worked with
must have seemed as thick
as ropes on ships, as cables
on a crane, but still their heads
would lower, their teeth bare
to nip away the raveled ends.

Only sometimes would they
lift their eyes to yours to show
how much lovelier than these twists

of silk and serge the garments
of the mind are, yet how much
more benign their implements
than mind's procedures
of forgiveness and repair.

And in your loneliness you'd notice
how really very gently they'd take
the fabric to its last, with what
solicitude gather up worn edges
to be bound, with what severe
but kind detachment wield
their amputating shears:
forgiveness, and repair.

Printed in the USA
CPSIA information can be obtained
at www.ICGtesting.com
LVHW091148150724
785511LV00005B/623